CONCERNING
DISSENT
AND
Civil Disobedience

CONCERNING
DISSENT
AND
Civil Disobedience

BY
ABE FORTAS

ASSOCIATE JUSTICE
SUPREME COURT
OF THE UNITED STATES

AN  BOOK

THE WORLD PUBLISHING COMPANY
NEW YORK   CLEVELAND

PREFACE

I have written this little book because I think it is important that as many people as possible should understand the basic principles governing dissent and civil disobedience in our democracy.

In part, this book tries to present a statement of basic legal principles. In part, it is frankly a statement of a moral, ethical, or philosophical point of view about dissent and how it may properly—and effectively—be expressed.

In the discussion of the legal principles, I have undertaken the difficult (and perhaps daring) task of a simple statement. I have tried to avoid technicalities or subtleties that delight the lawyer, but make hard reading for the layman. As a consequence, there may be some oversimplification in this presentation for which I ask forgiveness.

CONTENTS

☆

[vii]

CONTENTS

PART THREE
THE REVOLT OF YOUTH

☆

CONCLUSION

CONCERNING
DISSENT
AND
Civil Disobedience

PART ONE

☆

WHAT IS THE LAW
of
DISSENT?

1.

THE PARADOX:
THE DUTY TO OBEY
AND TO DISOBEY

☆

"Obedience to law is the only path to Freedom."
—A PASSIM PROVERB

"I think that we should be men first, and subjects afterward."
—HENRY DAVID THOREAU

". . . liberty is to be free from restraint and violence from others, which cannot be where there is no law."
—JOHN LOCKE

". . . law is restraint and absence of restraint is anarchy."
—BENJAMIN CARDOZO

"Human history began with an act of disobedience—it is likely to end with an act of obedience."
—ERICH FROMM

I AM A MAN OF THE LAW. I HAVE DEDICATED MY-self to uphold the law and to enforce its commands. I fully accept the principle that each of us is subject to law; that each of us is bound to obey the law enacted by his government.

But if I had lived in Germany in Hitler's days, I hope I would have refused to wear an armband, to *Heil Hitler*, to submit to genocide. This I hope, although Hitler's edicts were law until allied weapons buried the Third Reich.

If I had been a Negro living in Birmingham or Little Rock or Plaquemines Parish, Louisiana, I hope I would have disobeyed the state laws that said that I might not enter the public waiting room in the bus station reserved for "Whites."

I hope I would have insisted upon going into the parks and swimming pools and schools which state or city law reserved for "Whites."

I hope I would have had the courage to disobey, although the segregation ordinances were presumably law until they were declared unconstitutional.

How, then, can I reconcile my profound belief in obedience to law and my equally basic need to disobey *these* laws? Is there a principle, a code, a theory to which a man, with honor and integrity, may subscribe? Or is it all a matter of individual judgment? Do we live in a trackless jungle? Is there, or is there not, a path that law and integrity mark out through the maze of tangled obligations and conflicting loyalties?

Above all, it is critically important for us to know whether violence is essential, lawlessness necessary—or whether there are effective alternatives.

2.

THE SIMPLICITIES:
THE RIGHT TO DISSENT
AND ITS LIMITATIONS

☆

"A function of free speech . . . is to invite dispute. It may indeed best serve its high purpose when it induces . . . unrest . . . or even stirs people to anger."
—MR. JUSTICE DOUGLAS

☆

The Right

IN THE UNITED STATES, UNDER OUR CONSTITUTION, the question is not "may I dissent?" or "may I oppose a law or a government?" I *may* dissent. I *may* criticize. I *may* oppose. Our Constitution and our courts guarantee this.

The question is: *"How* may I do so?"

Each of us owes a duty of obedience to law. This is a moral as well as a legal imperative. So, first, we must seek to know which methods of protest are lawful: What are the means of opposition and dissent that are permissible under our system of law and which, therefore, will not subject us to punishment by the state and will not violate our duty of obedience to law?

There is another question. Are there occasions when we, with moral justification, may resort to methods of dissent, such as direct disobedience of an ordinance, even though the methods are unlawful? This is the perplexing philosophical question with which I shall deal in Part II of this discussion.

From our earliest history, we have insisted that each of us is and must be free to criticize the government, however sharply; to express dissent and opposition, however brashly; even to advocate overthrow of the government itself. We have insisted upon freedom of speech and of the press and, as the First Amendment to the Constitution puts it, upon "the right of the people peaceably to assemble and to petition the Government for a redress of grievances."

[18]

I say, with confidence, that nowhere in the world—at no time in history—has freedom to dissent and to oppose governmental action been more broadly safeguarded than in the United States of America, today. I say this even though I recognize that occasionally our officials depart from freedom's path.

This right to dissent may be exercised by the use of written and spoken words; by acts, such as picketing, which are sometimes referred to as "symbolic speech" because they are means of communicating ideas and of reaching the mind and the conscience of others; and by "peaceable" mass assembly and demonstrations. Ultimately, the basic means of protest under our system is the ballot box: the right to organize and to join with others to elect new officials to enact and administer the law.

These freedoms have long been celebrated. Our history and literature, as well as our law reports and legislative records, are crowded with moving and eloquent language reiterating the sanctity of dissent and the sacredness of the right to express it freely.

Our record as a nation demonstrates the validity of our commitment to freedom.

We are a great nation, I think, largely because of our protection of the freedom to criticize, to dissent, to oppose, and to join with others in mass opposition—and to do these things powerfully and effectively.

• • •

☆

The Limitations

☆

THERE ARE LIMITATIONS, HOWEVER, EVEN ON THE freedom of speech. The state may prescribe reasonable regulations as to when and where the right to harangue the public or to assemble a crowd may be exercised. It may require a permit for a mass meeting. But it can't use this housekeeping power for any purpose except to reduce the public inconvenience which any large assemblage involves.

And it is not true that anyone may say what's on his mind anytime and anywhere. According to the famous dictum of Justice Holmes, no one may falsely cry "Fire" in a crowded theater and thereby cause a panic. This is so even though the person's action may have been prompted by the highest motives.

He may have been alarmed and outraged by the lack of proper regulations to deal with fires in public places. He may have exhausted all other means to bring about the reform. He may have shouted "Fire" in the crowded theater only after all other measures failed, and only to dramatize the need and to secure necessary governmental action in the public interest.

But good motives do not excuse action which will injure others. The individual's conscience does not give him a license to indulge individual conviction without regard to the rights of others.

The man distressed at the inadequacy of fire regulations may speak in the public square; he may print and circulate pamphlets; he may organize mass meetings and picketing for the same purpose. He may denounce the city fathers as dunces, corrupt tools of the landlords, or potential murderers of innocent people.

He may even be able to call upon the courts to compel the government to act as he thinks it should. Our system provides a uniquely wide range of remedies in the courts which the citizen may invoke against his government.

Eventually, he and others may vote the government out of office.

But—and here is the point—he may not use means of advancing his program which, under the circumstances, will cause physical injury to others or unreasonably interfere with them.

Most of us would agree with Holmes that freedom to speak does not include falsely crying "Fire" in a crowded theater and causing a panic, but the illustration does not solve the problem of defining the limits of permissible protest. Even with Holmes' help, the line between the permissible and the prohibited remains hard to draw.

Speech, including symbolic speech such as picketing, never exists in limbo. It always occurs in a particular place and in particular circumstances. Even if *what is said* does not create a "clear and present danger" of physical injury to others, the place where the speech is uttered, the size of the crowd, and the circumstances may convert the lawful into the unlawful.

For example, if the participants unlawfully prevent the movement of traffic or if they unlawfully and needlessly trespass on private property, the fact that their speech is constitutionally protected will not necessarily shield them from arrest for the traffic violation or the trespass. The words may not occasion punishment, but the attendant circumstances may.

Even the application of this simple proposition is difficult. In *Brown v. Louisiana,* the Supreme Court divided five to four on a question of this sort. CORE had decided to protest segregation of public library facilities in the parishes of East and West Feliciana and St. Helena, Louisiana. Negroes were excluded from the three libraries serving the parishes. The parishes operated two bookmobiles. One was red, the other blue. The red bookmobile served only white persons. The blue bookmobile served only Negroes. Residents of the parishes could receive library service by presenting registration cards. The cards issued to Negroes were stamped "Negro." A Negro holding a card could receive library service. But only from the blue bookmobile.

On a Saturday morning, during regular library hours, five adult Negro men, members of CORE, entered the segregated library building. They asked the librarian for a book: *The Story of the Negro* by Arna Bontemps. The librarian told them it was not on the shelves. They remained in the reading room as a protest against the segregation of the library. They were quiet and orderly. They were asked to leave. They politely refused.

CORE had given the sheriff advance notice of the proposed sit-in. The sheriff and some deputies arrived in ten or fifteen minutes from the time the men entered the library. The protesters were arrested. They were tried and convicted of disorderly conduct under a Louisiana statute.

On appeal, five of the nine members of the United States Supreme Court voted to set aside their conviction. There were differences of opinion even among the five as to the precise basis of the decision. The opinion which I wrote was joined only by the Chief Justice and Mr. Justice Douglas. It concluded that the protesters were engaged in the peaceful exercise of First Amendment rights. My opinion said that these rights clearly include the right to protest the unconstitutional segregation of public facilities by "silent and reproachful presence, in a place where the protestant has every right to be. . . ."

Justices Brennan and White agreed with the result that we reached, but wrote separate opinions. The five of us agreed, however, that the conviction of the protesters violated the Bill of Rights of the federal Constitution.

Four members of the Court disagreed. They

did not quarrel with the proposition that the Negroes were privileged to enter the segregated library building, or that they were entitled, as members of the public, to library service. But they thought that by remaining in the library as a protest after they had asked for a book and had been informed it was not available, the Negroes were expressing their protest in an inappropriate and unauthorized place, and, accordingly, their action was not protected by the First Amendment.

In the minority's view, eloquently expressed by Mr. Justice Black, the Negroes had no right to be in the library after they had completed their business. Remaining there after their library business was completed, according to the minority of the Justices, was not a constitutionally protected form of protest, even though they entered the premises lawfully, remained there during regular hours only, and peacefully and quietly expressed their protest against the segregation of the library itself.

In substance, the difference between the majority and minority turned on their respective judgments as to whether a peaceful, orderly protest is ever protected by the First Amendment if it is held in a public library. The majority said it is protected if it does not interfere with others and takes place when the protesters have a right to be present.

The result might very well have gone against the protesters if they had stayed in the library after the regular hours during which it was open to the public. If they had done so, a majority and not a minority of the Court might have agreed that this conduct was not constitutionally protected.

The fact that they were sitting-in to protest segregation might not have protected them if they had violated reasonable regulations applicable to all, without discrimination. Their sit-in would not then have been merely an instance of symbolic speech. It would have been symbolic speech accompanied by violation of a lawful and appropriate regulation designed reasonably to regulate the use of a public facility by everybody.

· · ·

Burning draft cards or even American flags has been defended as a form of protest. Some people say that this should be permitted as symbolic speech. It is urged that it is nothing more than a picturesque or dramatic form of expressing protest.

But the problem is much more difficult than this. A punishable offense is not excused solely because the conduct is picturesque, even if its purpose (to protest) might be unassailable. As my discussion of the library sit-in case shows, if the protest involves violation of a *valid law,* the fact that it was violated in a "good cause"—such as to protest segregation or war—will not ordinarily excuse the violator.

The law violation is excused only if the law which is violated (such as a law segregating a public library)—only if *that law itself* is unconstitutional or invalid. In the library sit-in case the protesters violated a segregation ordinance. This ordinance was unconstitutional and its violation could not be constitutionally punished. But if the law violated by the sit-in had been a lawful and reasonable regulation of library hours, the outcome might well have been different.

The burning of draft cards or American flags involves direct violation of law. Laws forbidding the burning or desecration of the national flag have existed for many years, and it is hardly likely that anyone would seriously contest their constitutionality or legality. In the case of draft cards, however, it has been vigorously urged that the federal law prohibiting mutilation or burning of draft cards serves no real purpose and was recently enacted by the Congress merely to punish dissent. For this reason, it is said, the law is an unconstitutional burden on the right of free speech. Therefore, it is argued, the draft card burning should not be held to involve a violation of law. A case involving this question is awaiting decision by the Supreme Court and I cannot comment upon it. But the point that I make is that if the law forbidding the burning of a draft card is held to be constitutional and valid, the fact that the card is burned as a result of noble and constitutionally protected motives is no help to the offender.

I can illustrate the principle involved by reference to a problem that has arisen a number of times in connection with mass picketing. In *Cox v. Louisiana,* the Supreme Court reversed convictions for mass picketing even though the demonstration took place just outside of the courthouse and cells where civil rights activists, previously arrested, were incarcerated. But if the demonstrators had insisted upon blocking access to the courthouse, or had entered its doors and disrupted the work going on in the courthouse in order to stage a demonstration inside, or had refused to march or demonstrate in a way that allowed pedestrian or auto traffic to proceed, the result might have been different. The fact that they were engaged in a protest would not give them immunity from arrest and prosecution for their law violation.

. . .

This necessarily brief and general discussion discloses the difficulty and subtlety of the legal issues involved in determining whether a particular form of protest is or is not protected by the Bill of Rights. The reason for the difficulty is that, unavoidably, the Constitution seeks to accommodate two conflicting values, each of which is fundamental: the need for freedom to speak freely, to protest effectively, to organize, and to demonstrate; and the necessity of maintaining order so that other people's rights, and the peace and security of the state, will not be impaired.

The types of protests and the situations in which they occur are of infinite variety, and it is impossible to formulate a set of rules which will strike the proper balance between the competing principles. The precise facts in each situation will determine whether the particular protest or activity is within the shelter of the First Amendment or whether the protesters have overstepped the broad limits in which constitutional protection is guaranteed. It is, accordingly, hazardous to set out general principles. But here are a few principles that in my opinion indicate the contours of the law in this subtle and complex field where the basic right of freedom conflicts with the needs of an ordered society:

• • •

(1) Our Constitution protects the right of protest and dissent within broad limits. It generously protects the right to organize people for protest and dissent. It broadly protects the right to assemble, to picket, to stage "freedom walks" or mass demonstrations, if these activities are peaceable and if the protesters comply with reasonable regulations designed to protect the general public without substantially interfering with effective protest.

(2) If any of the rights to dissent is exercised

with the intent to cause unlawful action (a riot, or assault upon others) or to cause injury to the property of others (such as a stampede for exits or breaking doors or windows), and if such unlawful action or injury occurs, the dissenter will not be protected. He may be arrested, and if properly charged and convicted of law violation, he will not be rescued by the First Amendment.

(3) If the right to protest, to dissent, or to assemble peaceably is exercised so as to violate valid laws reasonably designed and administered to avoid interference with others, the Constitution's guarantees will not shield the protester. For example, he may be convicted for engaging in marching or picketing which blocks traffic or for sitting-in in an official's office or in a public or private place and thereby preventing its ordinary and intended use by the occupant or others. It is difficult to generalize about cases of this sort, because they turn on subtleties of fact: for example, Did the public authorities confine themselves to requiring only that minimum restriction necessary to permit the public to go about its business? Were there facilities available for the protest which were reasonably adequate to serve the lawful purposes of the protesters,

and which could have been used without de-
priving others of the use of the public areas?

• • •

Despite the limits which the requirements
of an ordered society impose, the protected
weapons of protest, dissent, criticism, and peaceable assembly are enormously powerful. Largely
as a result of the use of these instruments by
Negroes, the present social revolution was
launched: by freedom marches; organized boy-
cotts; picketing and mass demonstrations; protest and propaganda. And by the use of the
powerful instruments of dissent by people opposed to the war in Vietnam—by dissent expressed in the press, from the pulpit, on public
platforms, and in the colleges and universities—
issues of vast consequence have been presented
with respect to the war in Vietnam, and, without
doubt, national decisions and the course of that
war have been affected.

The events of the past few years in this
nation dramatically illustrate the power of the
ordinary citizen, armed with the great rights to
speak, to organize, to demonstrate. It would be
difficult to find many situations in history where

so much has been accomplished by those who, in cold realism, were divorced from the conventional instruments of power. Negroes and the youth-generation held no office. They did not control political machines. They did not own vast newspapers or magazines or radio or television stations. But they have caused great events to occur. They have triggered a social revolution which has projected this nation, and perhaps the world, to a new plateau in the human adventure. They have forced open the frontier of a new land—a land in which it is possible that the rights and opportunities of our society may be available to all, not just to some, in which the objectives of our Constitution may be fully realized for all; and in which the passion and determination of youth may be brought to the aid of our pursuit of the marvelous ideals that our heritage prescribes.

How wonderful it is that freedom's instruments—the rights to speak, to publish, to protest, to assemble peaceably, and to participate in the electoral process—have so demonstrated their power and vitality! These are our alternatives to violence; and so long as they are used forcefully but prudently, we shall continue as a vital, free society.

3.

THE RIGHTS OF THE STATE AND ITS DUTY IN WAR AS WELL AS PEACE

☆

"Must a government, of necessity, be too strong for the liberties of its own people, or too weak to maintain its own existence?"
—ABRAHAM LINCOLN

☆

SO THE CITIZEN HAS THE RIGHT, PROTECTED BY the Constitution, to criticize, however intemperately; to protest, however strongly; to draw others to his cause; and in mass, peaceably to assemble. The state must not only respect these rights and refrain from punishing their exercise but it must also protect the dissenter against

[35]

other citizens who seek by force, harassment, or interference to prevent him from exercising these rights. The state is obliged, if needed, to send police or state troopers to protect the mass march of people who are protesting against the state itself. This happened in the famous Selma march.

In theory, these great freedoms are protected even in wartime. As Justice Davis, speaking for the Supreme Court, wrote in 1866:

> The Constitution of the United States is a law for rulers and people, equally in war and in peace, and covers with the shield of its protection all classes of men, at all times, and under all circumstances. No doctrine, involving more pernicious consequences, was ever invented by the wit of man than that any of its provisions can be suspended during any of the great exigencies of government. Such a doctrine leads directly to anarchy or despotism. . . .

In practice, we have not always lived up to this theory. War tends to breed its own imperatives. War tends to create danger or the fear of danger to the state, and the state is always apt to respond to fear by taking measures which its officials consider necessary for its defense, and which sometimes are far more drastic than is justified.

In the Civil War, Abraham Lincoln, a great and sensitive President, presided over the arrest of more than thirteen thousand persons who had discouraged enlistment or otherwise were thought to have furnished aid and comfort to the enemy of the federal forces. At least twenty-one newspapers were suppressed, some expressly for "disloyal and incendiary statements."

During World War I, under another outstanding President, Woodrow Wilson, two sedition laws were enacted and more than fifteen hundred persons were arrested under their terms. Heavy sentences were imposed on some of the dissenters. The producer of a movie on the American Revolution was sentenced to ten years' imprisonment because his picture was found capable of arousing anti-British feelings.

In World War II, we needlessly and ruthlessly interned 117,000 Americans of Japanese ancestry—an act which will forever be a blot upon this nation's record.

It was during the Korean War—in the bitterness left by the Communist takeover in China—that McCarthyism was born, and the systematic blighting of thousands of lives and the destruction of valuable careers took place. Only a few of those whom McCarthyism injured had opposed this nation's wartime program or subscribed to Communism. Most of them were people who at some time had harbored ideas which were in conflict with the orthodoxy that McCarthy and his associates sought to impose on the nation—an orthodoxy which a helpless government and timid nation did not repudiate until a great many of our finest scholars and public officials had been brutally slandered and the national resource which they represented had been seriously depleted.

In the Vietnam war, except for occasional lapses like the Selective Service effort to reclassify and draft students for taking part in antiwar or antidraft demonstrations, the truth of the matter is that, to the date of this writing, there has been a remarkable absence of governmental effort to curtail the right to dissent and protest.

It is the courts—the independent judiciary —which have, time and again, rebuked the legislatures and executive authorities when, under the stress of war, emergency, or fear of Communism or revolution, they have sought to suppress the rights of dissenters. In the famous case of Exparte Milligas, the Supreme Court held that President Lincoln's suspension of the civil courts and the writ of habeas corpus were unconstitutional.

Although we were in a desperate war against Nazi Germany, the Supreme Court in 1943 reversed the conviction of persons who distributed literature condemning the war and the draft and opposing the flag salute. (*Taylor v. Mississippi,* 319 U.S. 583.)

Time and again, the Court has rebuked and rejected efforts to deprive people of their jobs in state and federal governments for their mere beliefs or mere membership in unpopular or even essentially subversive groups.

The Court has insisted upon freedom to speak and to organize, even if the object is ultimately subversive. Although the Communist party is devoted to overthrowing the government of the United States by force and violence, the Supreme Court has ruled that even an organizer for that party may not be jailed merely for recruiting members for the party.

But this obviously does not mean that the state must tolerate anything and everything that includes opposition to the government or to government law or policy. It does not mean that the courts will protect the dissident if the method of dissent involves aggression—something more than speech or symbolic speech for the communication of ideas to persuade others, or more than mere membership in a subversive organization. The state may and should act if the protest includes action directed at carrying out an attempt to overthrow the government by force or violence; or if it involves physical assault upon, or substantial interference with, the rights of others, or ordinarily trespass upon private property which is not open to the public.

In these situations, principles that are designed to protect the interest of the people generally in preserving the state come into play: The Constitution does not protect subversive acts. It does not shield sabotage. It does not tolerate espionage, theft of national secrets, or interference with the preparation of the nation's defense or its capacity to wage war. It does not protect these, however sincere the offender may be or however lofty his motives.

The state may defend its existence and its functions, not against words or argument or criticism, however vigorous or ill-advised, but against *action;* and the state may and must protect its citizens against injury, damage to their property, and willful and unnecessary disruption of their work and normal pursuits.

In our system, the courts have the ultimate responsibility of striking the balance between the state's right to protect itself and its citizens, and the individual's right to protest, dissent, and oppose. In the sense that I have described, neither of these rights is absolute. We have entrusted the courts with the task of striking the balance in individual cases, on the basis of principles stated in the Constitution in terms which are necessarily general and which leave room for differences of opinion—even among Justices of the Supreme Court.

In some systems of government, the only way to resolve the clash between the state and the individual is by force. In such confrontations, the state is almost certain to win. It imposes its will because it has the power and the force to do so. The citizen's only alternative, usually hopelessly remote, is to marshal enough strength from within and outside his country to overthrow the government.

In this country, however, we have many alternatives to the use of force. The citizen may bring pressure to bear on the state by writing, speaking, organizing, picketing, and demonstrating. He may, in many instances, bring suit against the state or its officials. The courts are generally available to the individual citizen when he claims that he is acting within his constitutional rights and that the state is wrongly interfering with him.

Under our system, as soon as the legal process is initiated, the state and the individual are equals. The courts are not instruments of the executive or legislative branches of the government. They are totally independent—subordinate only to the Constitution and to the rule of law.

When we stop to reflect upon it, this is a remarkable conception: that the individual citizen may protest governmental actions; that he may bitterly dissent from government policies; that he may oppose the government itself. Sometimes he may institute an action in court against the government. This is the way that the Negroes presented for decision their complaint that schools were segregated. Their actions led to the famous case of *Brown v. Board of Education,* in which the Court held that state-maintained segregation of public schools was unconstitutional.

If the government believes a citizen has

violated the law, as I have described, it may proceed against him by arrest and prosecution. But if it does so, the citizen and the state are on terms of equality to advocate their contentions before an impartial court: the citizen to claim that what he has done is within his constitutional right to speak and protest; the state to assert that he has exceeded the constitutional protections.

Our law even insists upon certain measures to equalize the contest and to assure that, as near as may be, the citizen and the state have equality of opportunity to present their respective contentions. If the state seeks to prosecute him for a serious crime, the citizen is guaranteed elaborate procedural rights. He cannot be made to testify against himself. If he is indigent, the state must, even at its own expense, provide him with a lawyer to defend him against the state and must give him certain facilities to prosecute an appeal if he loses.

Viewing the total situation, then, I think it is difficult to find fault with the theory of our system if one believes in the rules of ordered society. Mistakes are made; injustices are perpetrated. Sometimes the balance is struck so that the exercise of freedom is excessively restricted

—or even so that the state is inadequately protected (some people think this is the case with respect to decisions of the Supreme Court protecting procedural rights of persons accused of violating the law).

But the theory—the structure—of our system allows full opportunity for both the state and the individual to assert their respective claims and to have them adjudicated by impartial, independent tribunals, on the basis of a principle which is fundamental to our society: that freedom to criticize, to persuade, to protest, to dissent, to organize, and to assemble peaceably are as essential to vital, effective government as they are to the spiritual and material welfare of the individual; and that the exercise of this freedom will be protected and encouraged and may not be diminished so long as the form of its exercise does not involve action which violates laws prescribed to protect others in their peaceful pursuits, or which incites a clear and present danger of violence or injury to others.

PART TWO

☆

CIVIL
DISOBEDIENCE

4.

CIVIL DISOBEDIENCE

☆

*"A fanatic is one who redoubles his
efforts when he has forgotten his ends."*
—GEORGE SANTAYANA

*"To break the law of the land is always
serious, but it is not always wrong."*
—ROBERT BOLT

*"Is nonviolence, from your point of view,
a form of direct action?" inquired
Dr. Thurman. "It is not one form, it is
the only form," said Gandhi.*

☆

AT THE BEGINNING OF THIS BOOK, I SAID THAT IF
I had been a Negro in the South, I hope I would
have disobeyed the state and local laws denying
to Negroes equal access to schools, to voting
rights, and to public facilities. If I had disobeyed those laws, I would have been arrested

and tried and convicted. Until the Supreme Court ruled that these laws were unconstitutional, I would have been a law violator.

As it turned out, my refusal to obey those laws would have been justified by the courts. But suppose I had been wrong. Suppose the Supreme Court had decided that the laws were constitutional. Despite the deep moral conviction that motivated me—despite the fact that my violation of the discriminatory racial laws would have been in a great cause—I would have been consigned to jail, with no possible remedy except the remote prospect of a pardon.

This may seem harsh. It may seem especially harsh if we assume that I profoundly believe that the law I am violating is immoral and unconstitutional, or and if we assume that the question of its constitutionality is close. *But this is what we mean by the rule of law:* both the government and the individual must accept the result of procedures by which the courts, and ultimately the Supreme Court, decide that the law is such and such, and not so and so; that the law has or has not been violated in a particular situation, and that it is or is not constitutional; and that the individual defendant has or has not been properly convicted and sentenced.

This is the rule of law. The state, the courts, and the individual citizen are bound by a set of laws which have been adopted in a prescribed manner, and the state and the individual must accept the courts' determinations of what those rules are and mean in specific instances. *This is the rule of law,* even if the ultimate judicial decision is by the narrow margin of five to four!

The term "civil disobedience" has been used to apply to a person's refusal to obey a law which the person believes to be immoral or unconstitutional. John Milton's famous defiance of England's law requiring licensing of books by official censors is in this category. He openly announced that he would not comply with it. He assailed the censorship law as an intolerable restriction of freedom, contrary to the basic rights of Englishmen.

The phrase "civil disobedience" has been grossly misapplied in recent years. Civil disobedience, even in its broadest sense, does not apply to efforts to overthrow the government or to seize control of areas or parts of it by force, or by the use of violence to compel the government to grant a measure of autonomy to part of its population. These are programs of revolution. They are not in the same category as the programs of reformers who—like Martin Luther King—seek changes within the established order.

Revolutionists are entitled, of course, to the full benefit of constitutional protections for the *advocacy* of their program. They are even protected in the many types of *action* to bring about a fundamental change, such as the organization of associations and the solicitation of members and support at the polls. But they are not protected in the use of violence. Programs of this sort, if they are pursued, call for law enforcement by police action. They are not likely to raise issues of the subtlety of those with which I am here concerned.

This kind of violent action is in sharp contrast with the theory of civil disobedience which, even where it involves a total or partial repudiation of the principle that the individual should obey the law, does not tolerate violent methods. Thoreau presents an example of a general refusal to accept the authority of the state. Thoreau said he would pay certain taxes—for example, for roads—but not a general tax, to a government which tolerated slavery. Thoreau rejected the proposition that the individual must support all governmental activities, even those which he vigorously opposes. Thoreau asserted the right to choose which taxes he would pay; to decide for himself that this was a morally justified tax and that certain others were not. Government, he said, "can have no pure right over my person and property but what I concede to it." Thoreau's position was not far from that asserted by Joan Baez and others who refused to pay federal taxes which were used to finance the war in Vietnam. But Thoreau's position was less selective. His principle would apply to all acts of government except those which he approved.

The term "civil disobedience" has not been limited to protests in the form of refusal to obey a law because of disapproval of that particular law. It has been applied to another kind of civil disobedience. This is the violation of laws which the protester does not challenge because of their own terms or effect. The laws themselves are not the subject of attack or protest. They are violated only as a means of protest, like carrying a picket sign. They are violated in order to publicize a protest and to bring pressure on the public or the government to accomplish purposes which have nothing to do with the law that is breached. The great exponent of this type of civil disobedience was Gandhi. He protested the British rule in India by a general program of disobedience to the laws governing ordinary civil life.

The first type, as in Milton's case—the direct refusal to obey the specific law that is the subject of protest—may sometimes be a means, even an essential means, of testing the constitution-methods. Thoreau presents an example. Thoreau ality of the law. For example, a young man may be advised by counsel that he must refuse to report for induction in order to challenge the constitutionality of the Selective Service Act. This is very different from the kind of civil disobedience which is *not* engaged in for the purpose of testing the legality of an order within our system of government and laws, but which is practiced as a technique of warfare in a social and political conflict over other issues.

Frequently, of course, civil disobedience is prompted by both motives—by both a desire to make propaganda and to challenge the law. This is true in many instances of refusal to submit to induction. It was true in the case of Mrs. Vivian Kellems, who refused to pay withholding taxes because she thought they were unlawful and she wanted to protest the invasion of her freedom as a capitalist and citizen.

Let me first be clear about a fundamental

proposition. The motive of civil disobedience, whatever its type, does not confer immunity for law violation. Especially if the civil disobedience involves violence or a breach of public order prohibited by statute or ordinance, it is the state's duty to arrest the dissident. If he is properly arrested, charged, and convicted, he should be punished by fine or imprisonment, or both, in accordance with the provisions of law, unless the law is invalid in general or as applied.

He may be motivated by the highest moral principles. He may be passionately inspired. He may, indeed, be right in the eyes of history or morality or philosophy. These are not controlling. It is the state's duty to arrest and punish those who violate the laws designed to protect private safety and public order.

The Negroes in Detroit and Newark and Washington and Chicago who rioted, pillaged, and burned may have generations of provocation. They may have incontestable justification. They may have been pushed beyond endurance. In the riots following the assassination of Martin Luther King, Jr., the Negroes may have been understandably inflamed by the murder of their leading advocate of nonviolence. But that provides no escape from the consequences of their conduct. Rioters should be arrested, tried, and convicted. If the state does not do so, it is either because of a tactical judgment that arrest and prosecution would cause more harm than good, or because the state is incompetent.

The same principles apply to the police and officers of the law. They, too, are liable for their acts. The fact that they represent the state does not give them immunity from the consequences of brutality or lawlessness. They, like the rioters, may be motivated by long and acute provocation. It may be that their lawlessness was the direct product of fear, or of righteous anger. They may have been moved to violence by more pressure than they could endure. But they, too, are subject to the rule of law, and if they exceed the authorized bounds of firmness and self-protection and needlessly assaulted the people whom they encountered, they should be disciplined, tried, and convicted. It is a deplorable truth that because they are officers of the state they frequently escape the penalty for their lawlessness.

We are a government and a people under law. It is not merely *government* that must live under law. Each of us must live under law. Just as our form of life depends upon the government's subordination to law under the Constitution, so it also depends upon the individual's subservience to the laws duly prescribed. Both of these are essential.

Just as we expect the government to be bound by all laws, so each individual is bound by all of the laws under the Constitution. He cannot pick and choose. He cannot substitute his own judgment or passion, however noble, for the rules of law. Thoreau was an inspiring figure and a great writer; but his essay should not be read as a handbook on political science. A citizen cannot demand of his government or of other people obedience to the law, and at the same time claim a right in himself to break it by lawless conduct, free of punishment or penalty.

Some propagandists seem to think that people who violate the laws of public order ought not to be arrested and punished if their violation has protest as its purpose. By calling the criminal acts "civil disobedience," they seek to persuade us that offenses against public and private security should be immune from punishment and even commended. They seek to excuse physical attacks upon police; assaults upon recruiters for munitions firms and for the armed services; breaking windows in the Pentagon and in private stores and homes; robbing stores; trespassing on private and official premises; occupying academic offices; and even pillaging, looting, burning, and promiscuous violence.

We are urged to accept these as part of the First Amendment freedoms. We are asked to agree that freedom to speak and write, to protest and persuade, and to assemble provides a sanctuary for this sort of conduct. But that is nonsense.

The Supreme Court of the United States has said, over and over, that the words of the First Amendment mean what they say. But they mean what they say and not something else. They guarantee freedom to speak and freedom of the press—not freedom to club people or to destroy property. The First Amendment protects the right to assemble and to petition, but it requires—in plain words—that the right be peaceably exercised.

The use of force or violence in the course of social protest is a far cry from civil disobedience as practiced by Gandhi. Gandhi's concept insists upon peaceful, nonviolent refusal to comply with a law. It assumes that the protester will be punished, and it requires peaceful submission to punishment.

Let me elaborate this by reference to an article written by Dr. Martin Luther King, Jr., and published in September of 1961. In this article, Dr. King set forth the guiding principles of his approach to effective protest by civil disobedience. He said that many Negroes would disobey "unjust laws." These he defined as laws which a minority is compelled to observe but which are not binding on the majority. He said that this must be done openly and peacefully, and that those who do it must accept the penalty imposed by law for their conduct.

This is civil disobedience in a great tradition. It is peaceful, nonviolent disobedience of laws which are themselves unjust and which the protester challenges as invalid and unconstitutional.

Dr. King was involved in a case which illustrated this conception. He led a mass demonstration to protest segregation and discrimination in Birmingham. An injunction had been issued by a state court against the demonstration. But Dr. King disregarded the injunction and proceeded with the march as planned. He was arrested. He was prosecuted in the state court, convicted of contempt, and sentenced to serve five days in jail. He appealed, claiming that the First Amendment protected his violation of the injunction.

I have no doubt that Dr. King violated the injunction in the belief that it was invalid and his conduct was legally as well as morally justified. But the Supreme Court held that he was bound to obey the injunction unless and until it was set aside on appeal; and that he could not disregard the injunction even if he was right that the injunction was invalid. Dr. King went to jail and served his time.

I have no moral criticism to make of Dr. King's action in this incident, even though it turned out to be legally unjustified. He led a peaceable demonstration. He acted in good faith. There was good, solid basis for his belief that he did not have to obey the injunction—until the Supreme Court ruled the other way. The Court disagreed with him by a vote of five to four. I was one of the dissenters. Then Dr. King, without complaint or histrionics, accepted the penalty of misjudgment. This, I submit, is action in the great tradition of social protest in a democratic society where all citizens, including protesters, are subject to the rule of law.

But since those relatively early days of the

protest movement, discontent has greatly increased in volume and depth of feeling, and the tactics of the discontented—both of the Negroes and the antiwar and antidraft groups—have become more forceful and less restrained. We confront instances of riots, sporadic violence, and trespass. These call for police and law enforcement and do not present the problem with which we are concerned. But we are also faced with the prospect of mass civil disobedience. Unless the greatest care is exercised, programs of this sort can disrupt the life and work of major cities. Mass demonstrations like the March on Washington in 1963 can be staged with good effect, by careful preparation and discipline, on the basis of cooperative planning between the leaders of the demonstration and the city officials. They can take place without appreciable law violation, under absolute constitutional protection. But when they are characterized by action deliberately designed to paralyze the life of a city by disrupting traffic and the work of government and its citizens—they carry with them extreme danger.

The danger of serious national consequences from massive civil disobedience may easily be exaggerated. Our nation is huge and relatively dispersed. It is highly unlikely that protesters can stage a nationwide disruption of our life, comparable to the effects of a general strike such as France and other nations have witnessed. But a program of widespread mass civil disobedience, involving the disruption of traffic, movement of persons and supplies, and conduct of government business within any of our great cities, would put severe strains on our constitutional system.

These mass demonstrations, however peacefully intended by their organizers, always involve the danger that they may erupt into violence. But despite this, our Constitution and our traditions, as well as practical wisdom, teach us that city officials, police and citizens must be tolerant of mass demonstrations, however large and inconvenient. No city should be expected to submit to paralysis or to widespread injury to persons and property brought on by violation of law. It must be prepared to prevent this by the use of planning, persuasion, and restrained law enforcement. But at the same time, it is the city's duty under law, and as a matter of good sense, to make every effort to provide adequate facilities so that the demonstration can be effectively staged, so that it can be conducted without paralyzing the city's life, and to provide protection for the demonstrators. The city must perform this duty.

An enormous degree of self-control and discipline are required on both sides. Police must be trained in tact as well as tactics. Demonstrators must be organized, ordered, and controlled. Agitators and *provocateurs,* whatever their object, must be identified, and any move that they may make toward violence must be quickly countered.

However careful both sides may be, there is always danger that individual, isolated acts of a few persons will overwhelm the restraint of thousands. Law violation or intemperate behavior by one demonstrator may provoke police action. Intemperate or hasty retaliation by a single policeman may provoke disorder, and civil disobedience may turn into riot. This is the dangerous potential of mass demonstrations. When we add to it the possibility that extremists on either side are likely to be at work to bring about the cycle of disorder, arrest, resistance, and riot, the danger assumes formidable proportions.

5.

AN EVALUATION

☆

*". . . active resistance can be used
only as the very last resort in a
critical case, after all peaceful and
constitutional means have been
exhausted."*

—MAX PRIBILLA, S. J.

☆

OUR SOCIETY GAINED A GREAT DEAL FROM THE
powerful protests by and on behalf of the Negro.
These protests awakened the nation's conscience
to an intolerable situation: the continued denial,
a hundred years after the abolition of slavery, of
fundamental rights and equal opportunity to
millions of our citizens. We were jolted to awareness of the moral and political disease of segregation and discrimination which threatened to de-

stroy us as a great and decent nation.

But this social revolution, like almost all revolutions, has an implacable rhythm of its own. The conscience of white America quickly responds to the accusation of guilt. *Mea culpa* comes readily to our lips, and we react quickly and generously. But in a social revolution, the demands for action, for cure, for restitution, for reparation, are not easily met. The demand is not satisfied by initial or moderate response. It is fed by it. The vigor and fervor of the demand increase as its justice is admitted and some steps are taken to meet it. As demand outstrips the early response, attitudes on both sides harden. Frustration sets in. Those demanding change see no prospect of satisfaction; those who initially offered reform despair of a reasonable resolution. And so, conflict and crisis occur.

At best, it will take generations to repair the ravages of past neglect and oppression of the Negroes. The size of the job to be done, the nature of the rehabilitation to be undertaken, mean that the Negroes who are now grown— scarred, embittered, and deprived—will not be restored to full dignity and health. They can expect at best only something of a job, something somewhat better as a home. But they can expect

[64]

and should demand a better life so far as their children and, especially, their children's children are concerned.

So we must expect to live, if not with the apartheid of which the President's Riot Commission warns, with continued friction. The needs cannot be met in our lifetime. The shape of things to come will be determined by the tone and level of the Negro protest movement, the white community's response, and the interaction of the two. Unremitting pressure, peaceably applied by the Negro community, will undoubtedly expedite response. Effective organization, demonstrated at the polls, will be of enormous help. But Negro violence will be met by police violence and the violence of the white population; and their violence will inspire further Negro aggressions.

The Negroes have gained much by the strength of their protests and the massiveness of their demonstrations. Even their riots—much as we dislike acknowledging it—produced some satisfaction of their demands, some good response as well as some that was negative. But the reaction to repeated acts of violence may be repression instead of remedy. Riot produces fear; and fear has a tendency to still the response of conscience, which, although it may be quick to sound, is nevertheless a still, small voice, easily overcome by the strident notes of violence.

Negroes have acquired in this revolutionary process some solid instruments of solid advance. The very fact that they have been able to unite and, as a united people, bravely to assert their rights by vigorous protest and demonstration, has been a miracle. It has given them, in their own esteem and in the estimation of others, dignity and quality which are of the utmost significance to their progress and the nation's welfare. They have acquired the all-important access to the ballot box. They have achieved positions of importance and influence in our governments, state and federal. They have found solidarity and dignity.

They have discovered that they can mass their strength and pool their protests and achieve great benefits. They have induced the establishment to accept Negroes in its highest offices. These Negroes are obtaining invaluable training as lawyers, government officials, educators, business executives, and administrators. While some of these will be assimilated in their outlook and will lose their separate value to the Negro cause, some will be a source of new and more skillful leadership and of inspiration to the younger generations.

Given time and continued, vigorous use of constitutional instruments of dissent and protest and mass demonstration, the Negroes will move forward. They will force the white community to complete the job of reparation which has been begun. But widespread violence—whether it is civil disobedience, or street riots, or guerrilla warfare—will, I am persuaded, lead to repression. It will provide the white community with a reason for refusing to endure the discomfort and burden of the vast job of restitution and reparation.

In the last analysis, it is not the physical power of the Negro that is forcing the white community to undertake this job, but the moral power of his cause. It is basically conscience, justice, and a long and entirely justified view of national interest that impel the white majority to move to rectify an intolerable situation.

Violence on the part of a minority is sometimes a means of producing quick recognition of needs. It is not a productive technique for inducing the majority to undertake a job that must be figured in years of time and billions of dollars.

[67]

I recognize that there are times and societies in which violence employed to accomplish political ends has been respected. In times long gone by, tyrannicide had its respectable defenders. George Washington and friends were violent revolutionists. It is certainly arguable that slavery was abolished only by force of arms. But these analogies are too facile.

Violence is never defensible—and it has never succeeded in securing massive reform in an open society where there were *alternative methods of winning the minds of others to one's cause and securing changes in the government or its policies*. In the United States these avenues are certainly available. Our history and, specifically, the remarkable story of the present social revolution show that the alternatives of organization and protest (protected by the First Amendment), and of access to the ballot box, are open and effective. They may be long processes. They may be difficult. But they can produce lasting results. The alternative of violent methods employed by a minority can achieve the spurious appearance of temporary successes, but it will defeat the realistic objective: a long, difficult, burdensome program of reparation and rehabilitation of the Negro community.

PART THREE

☆

THE REVOLT
of
YOUTH

6.

THE RULES

☆

"Since inside of Me there is a Person, why
should he not share the shaping of
my life and of the world in which
I must live?"
—A YOUTH REFLECTION

☆

THE PRINCIPLES THAT I'VE DISCUSSED APPLY, OF
course, to the revolt of the youth-generation—of
the sixteen- to twenty-five-year-olds—as well as to
the social revolution. They apply to the white
collegian as well as to the Negro resident of
the ghetto.

The revolt of the young people, on and
off the campus, is a fairly new phenomenon
for this country. Our young people have been
submissive, hedonistic, and practical-minded.

Their idealism has been largely confined to dreams, poetry, and abstractions. Even in the depths of the Depression, relatively few of them were activists. They have accepted the leadership of their elders, not uncritically, but passively. Their revolt has usually taken the form of social misbehavior, not of political activism.

Until the generation of John F. Kennedy, their participation in practical politics was marked by acceptance of "junior" status: The Junior Chamber of Commerce, the Young Democrats, etc. Only a few years ago, in President Eisenhower's administration, many of us despaired because the college generation was so passive, so docile, and so uninvolved. It was apparently uninterested in anything that was not safe, conventional, and serviceable in practical terms.

Now this has drastically changed. Young people have suddenly taken on distinctive character and quality. They are not merely junior-size editions of their elders. They have become a positive, differentiated factor in American life. They are no longer predictably proceeding in a straight line behind their parents and grandparents, preparing to receive the torch from their elders to run the next lap in the old relay race.

This refusal to accept the existing pattern of life and thought merely because it exists is, I think, the common element in the revolt of the youth-generation. I do not suggest that most of this age group are active, conscious participants in the revolt. A sharp change in the philosophy of life of a generation is always the work of a few, although it may influence the destiny of all. Probably a majority of today's young people are going about their lives with little discernible difference between their basic actions and those of their parents' generation. But the existence of a special, independent outlook and orientation of the youth-generation is an article of faith to which most of them subscribe. Even though it is ill-defined, hazy in outline, and uncertain in context, the revolt profoundly affects the lives of all of them—even of those who do not participate in the new activities.

This refusal to accept the domination of the past—the insistence upon this generation's right and duty to make its own life-decisions—has produced both count-me-outs and count-me-ins. It has produced the hippies, the psychedelic addicts, and the flower-children. It has also produced other young people, not so picturesque in their appearance or habits, who have quietly divorced themselves from the mainstream of life. These are the count-me-outs who decline to join in the agony and activity of their time, or in its customary preoccupations. They are immersed in the warm fluid of me-ness. They reject a world which they regard as crass or callous.

On the other hand, there are the activists, the militants, who are passionately devoted to the cause of the Negroes and the poor, and to promoting student domination of university management, and to such causes as opposition to the war in Vietnam and to the draft. They participate vigorously in the life around them to advance those causes. These are the count-me-ins. They have ideas, programs, convictions, energy, and initiative. Some of them were significant participants in the freedom rides and marches and the early struggle to end discrimination against Negroes. They organize and participate in mass activities to achieve their objectives and to defeat governmental and university actions which they oppose.

Many reasons have contributed to the youth revolt: the affluence of our society and the resulting removal of the pressure to prepare oneself for economic survival; the deterioration of the family unit; the increasing involvement of universities and their faculties with nonteaching interests; the disruptive shock of the atom bomb, which gave a new uncertainty and instability to life; the prospect that their lives will be interrupted by compulsory military service; the opposition to the war in Vietnam; the shock of discovering that our national pride and progress concealed the misery and degradation in which Negroes and the poor were living; disillusionment with the standards of the older generation; the new awareness of the wretched state of most of the world's people which came with the end of colonialism; the example of Negroes in this country and of the people of Africa and Asia, who by individual and group effort, courage, and organization, have fought and sometimes won heroic battles.

Most of all, the revolt has found impetus, reason, and outlet in the opposition to the war in Vietnam and to the draft. Many of the younger generation, as well as some of their elder (justifiably or not), have come to regard this as a war of a small people against oppression by a vast power, as a struggle for national unity, or as a purely civil war in which our country is "brutally" participating. This has reinforced the natural and familiar opposition of many young men to military service, and especially to compulsory military service. In the minds of these

young people, the draft is bad enough; but to
be drafted to fight a war which they are led to
believe is disreputable, is intolerable.

The disaffection of youth is expressed by a
great variety of activities, ranging from the
amusingly juvenile to formidable, threatening
assaults upon the institutions of our society. It
is difficult for the young people who are moved
to passionate action by these factors to resign
themselves to the idea that they may be punished
if their actions violate the law. They *know* they
are right. They are certain that their motives
are pure. And they do not accept the proposition
that there is any virtue in obedience to authority.
They are not broken to society's bridle.

Negroes and poor people are more likely
than the young to have experienced conflict with
law and police. They are more likely to accept
the fact that transgression of the rules carries
with it the penalty of punishment. They may
not like the consequences, but they do not react
with the sense of injustice that the campus "rad-
ical" feels. He knows that he is both righteous
and right. Generally, his background is middle-
class and "respectable." It is impossible for him
really to visualize a confrontation between himself and the power of the law. He cannot really

see himself as a "criminal," even if he starts a scuffle with the police, destroys property, or assaults persons engaged in recruiting for the armed forces or war industries.

But the rules apply to him as well as to the Negroes and the indigent. The college youth who is protesting against the college administration or the war in Vietnam or the draft has, of course, the full scope of First Amendment rights. He is entitled to the full protection of the state and the courts in the exercise of speech and symbolic speech, however hostile. But he is not entitled to immunity if he directly and willfully incites violence or insists upon deliberately disrupting the work or movement of others.

A university may choose to refrain from complaining to the police if students disrupt classes by physical violence, or destroy university property, or manhandle recruiters for the armed services or for industries making war materials. If it does not take action itself or summon police assistance, the police are not likely to take the initiative on the campus. But if it lodges a complaint, the governing legal principles in this country are not essentially different from those applicable off campus.

Campus and university facilities are public

facilities; but public use does not authorize either the general public or the university faculty and students to use them in a way which subverts their purpose and prevents their intended use by others. The public character of a university does not grant to individuals a license to engage in activities which disrupt the activities to which those facilities are dedicated.

I know of no legal principle which protects students on campus from the consequences of activities which would be violations of law if undertaken elsewhere. This is the law, but we are now confronted with a problem which is not solved by mechanical application of the criminal law: the problem of readjusting campus life to the new attitudes and demands, and of coping with the disaffections which afflict so many students.

Here again, perhaps it is a beginning to separate student activities which are nonviolent from those which involve assault or damage to persons or property. Where the law violation is nonviolent or technical (such as blocking entrance to a campus building, or even orderly occupancy of a university facility), there may be sense in patient forbearance despite the wrong that the action involves. But violent activities, in my judgment, should be regarded and treated as intolerable. Punishment of on-campus violence involves risks. Particularly in respect to the youth-generation, it should be undertaken only after all efforts to persuade, patiently applied, have been exhausted. But the toleration of violence involves, I think, even greater risks, not only of present damage and injury but of erosion of the base of an ordered society. The point, I think, is not whether the aggressor should be halted and punished, but how; and it is here that moderation, consideration, and sympathetic understanding should play their part.

I do not know how profound in intensity or how lasting the current youth revolt may be. It may presage a new and welcome era of idealism in the nation. It may forecast the development of greater maturity and independence of outlook among our young people, and this may be productive of much good. It may even bring about the development of increased maturity in the educational and living rules of our colleges. In any event, it presents a challenge to the older generations as well as to youth to reconsider the goals of our society and its values, and urgently to reappraise the distribution of function and responsibility among the generations.

7.

THE DRAFT AND THE WAR IN VIETNAM

☆

"A well-regulated militia being necessary to the security of a free State . . . ."
—BILL OF RIGHTS, ARTICLE II

"Thou shalt not kill."
—THE BOOK OF EXODUS

"Not every difference of policy is a difference of principle."
—THOMAS JEFFERSON

☆

Conscientious Objectors

YOUTH'S DISAFFECTION FINDS ITS MOST DRAMATIC expression in the widespread opposition to the draft and the war in Vietnam. The right of the government to compel service in the armed

[81]

forces is based upon Article I, Section 8, of the Constitution, which authorizes the Congress to raise armed forces. From time immemorial, service in the armed forces, however onerous and distasteful, has been regarded as an obligation which the state may impose because of citizenship or residence.

From colonial times, however, there has been in this country general acceptance of the principle that while "conscientious objectors" are not exempt from the draft, they should not be forced into combat service. The special treatment of conscientious objectors was a natural and necessary corollary of our dedication to religious freedom. The exemption of conscientious objectors from combat service was debated in the Constitutional Convention, but it was not expressly written into the Constitution. It has been contended that the Constitution, because of the guarantees of religious freedom in the First Amendment, requires the exemption. But this has never been judicially established. The exemption has been included by the Congress in the various draft acts, and the decisions of the Supreme Court implementing the exemption have turned upon the construction of the statutory language.

Congress has stated the conscientious objector exemption in different terms at different times. The first Federal Conscription Law, enacted in 1863, did not refer to conscientious objectors, but it provided an escape from the draft. An individual could supply an acceptable substitute for himself or pay three hundred dollars to the War Department to use in procuring a substitute.

In the 1864 Draft Act, it was provided that persons who were "conscientiously opposed" to bearing arms and were prohibited from doing so by the articles of their "religious denomination," could secure exemption from combat. They then had the choice of hospital duty or of paying three hundred dollars to be applied to the benefit of sick and wounded soldiers.

The 1917 Draft Act restated the exemption and made it available to members of "any well-recognized religious sect" whose creed or principles forbade its members to "participate in war in any form." It eliminated the possibility of payment, but required noncombatant service as the President might prescribe. The Draft Act of 1940 eliminated the requirement of adherence to a recognized religious sect and granted exemption from combat to any person who by reason of "religious training and belief" was conscientiously opposed to war in any form.

Presently, the language is as follows:

> (j) Nothing contained in this title shall be construed to require any person to be subject to combatant training and service in the armed forces of the United States who, by reason of religious training and belief, is conscientiously opposed to participation in war in any form. Religious training and belief in this connection means an individual's belief in a relation to a Supreme Being involving duties superior to those arising from any human relation, but does not include essentially political, sociological, or philosophical views or a merely personal moral code.

The statute provides that the conscientious objector should be assigned to noncombatant service, or, if he is conscientiously opposed to participation even in that service, to "work of national importance under civilian direction."

In the famous Seeger case, decided in 1965, the Supreme Court had to consider whether the combat exemption was limited to persons who opposed war because of religious belief in the conventional sense—that is, centering upon belief in a Supreme Being. The Court ruled that the statutory provision could not be so restricted. It held that it also extended to persons who held a profound "belief that is sincere and meaningful" which "occupies a place in the life of its possessor parallel to that filled by the orthodox belief in God of one who clearly qualifies for the exemption."

This ruling equated profound moral beliefs with orthodox religious convictions for purposes of conscientious-objector status. But it did not modify the statute's admonition that the special status "does not include essentially political, sociological, or philosophical views or a merely personal moral code."

The principle of special status for conscientious objectors has never been extended to persons whose opposition to war is based only on intellectual grounds: for example, that war aids neither the victor nor the vanquished. As the Seeger decision emphasizes, the conscientious objection must proceed from a basic, general, moral philosophy or religious commitment which involves, as the statute says, opposition "to participation in war in any form." It has not been extended to persons whose moral conviction is that a particular war, rather than war generally, is abhorrent.

The needs of the state for manpower to wage war are always critical. Its ability to muster the needed soldiers may be the measure of its ability to survive. Even so, our government, as well as other states that reflect the ideals of civilization, recognizes and has always recognized that an individual's fundamental moral or religious commitments are entitled to prevail over the needs of the state. As Chief Justice Hughes said many years ago: "When one's belief collides with the power of the State, the latter is supreme within its sphere . . . But, in the forum of conscience, duty to a moral power higher than the State has always been maintained."

Relatively few of our people subscribe to a fundamental, philosophical, or religious rejection of all war. Despite all of the current clamor, as of 1966, conscientious objectors amounted to substantially less than 1 percent of all registrants in the Selective Service System. Most of our people recognize war as a savage inevitability in a world which is still far from being universally civilized.

Many of our young people, however, profoundly object to our participation in the war in Vietnam. Many of them say that our participation is "immoral"; and some believe that they should not be subject to induction or, if drafted, should be given conscientious-objector (noncombat) status because of their conscientious belief that our participation in this particular war is "immoral."

The attitude of these persons is entitled to respect, whether or not one agrees with it. It is not at all the same as that of the relatively few who sacrifice their self-respect by falsely claiming basic moral or religious objections to all war, which, if true, would entitle them to noncombat status. These persons, and those who counsel them in a self-degrading deceit, are not entitled to serious consideration. But that is not true of the thousands of young men who are seriously and honestly wrestling with the dilemma of rejecting not all wars, but their deep moral aversion to participation in a particular war.

We may respect their sincerity and sympathize with their problem, but in fact their claim that their profound rejection of a particular war should prevail over the state's needs is hardly consistent with the basic theory of organized society. By participating in the particular war, the state takes the position that the war *is* justified and moral. This is a governmental decision of the utmost gravity, and while the state can and should defer to the principle that a citizen may be excused from full participation in its consequences because of his duty "to a moral (or religious) power higher than the state," the state cannot acknowledge an individual's right to veto its decision that a particular war is right and necessary.

From the state's viewpoint, a disagreement about the morality of a particular war is a difference of judgment or policy; it is not and cannot be accepted as stemming from a moral or religious belief. In his First Inaugural Address, Jefferson said, "Not every difference of policy is a difference of principle." Once the state's decision has been made, and so long as the government adheres to it, it is not possible to exempt from its impact an individual who disagrees with that decision on the basis of a moral or intellectual judgment, as contrasted with an individual who is pledged to a general religious or moral philosophy which rejects war.

If the individual can veto his participation in the Vietnam war, he could also have declined to participate in World War II or the Korean conflict or a defense against invasion. This ability of the individual to choose his war, from the state's viewpoint, would destroy the state's ability to defend itself or to perform the obligations it has assumed, or to prevent the spread of attempts to conquer other nations of the world by outside-inspired and -aided subversion. The government having made this decision, the theory of the state insists that the individual must conform his conduct to it until the government's position is changed by congressional action or at the ballot box, or, indeed, by the persuasion of argument, protest, mass demonstration, and other methods safeguarded by the First Amendment.

Most of our wars have met bitter and violent condemnation as "immoral" and "barbarous." In the Revolutionary War, only about half of the people supported the revolution. Churchmen led the vocal opposition. Wealthy families bitterly assailed the politicians like George Washington whom they charged with base and selfish motivation.

The War of 1812 was at first supported by a majority of the people. But in a short while, as we encountered difficulties and reverses, opposition became rampant. The nation had at first agreed that the war was necessary to prevent British depredations. However, after a time the war was attacked throughout New England as "without justifiable cause and prosecuted in a

manner which indicates that conquest and am-
bition are its real motives." Men and money
were refused for the prosecution of the war. It
was denounced by such persons as Chief Justice
Marshall, Josiah Quincy, John Randolph of
Virginia, William Ellery Channing, and William Cullen Bryant.

While the British army was at the very gates
of New Orleans, the Hartford Convention was
called to protest the war. This Convention included persons bearing the distinguished family
names of Cabot, Lowell, Dwight, Lyman, Bige-
low, Longfellow. The Governor of Massachu-
setts sent three commissioners to Washington to
take the surrender, so he said, of a beaten administration and a defeated country. But while
they were on their way, Jackson won the battle
of New Orleans and the Treaty of Ghent was
signed. There was an immediate reversal of
public opinion. The Federalist party, which had
opposed the war, soon disappeared.

The Mexican War was also popular at the
start. But as it dragged on, it was bitterly denounced. Whig journals told Mexico that "her
cause was just, that a majority of Americans de-
tested the war, that our treasury could not bear
the cost, that our government was incompetent

. . . that our armies could not win the war, and that soon the Administration would be rebuked and its policies reversed." Congress passed a resolution condemning the war. Senator Webster charged President Polk with an "impeachable offense" in conducting the war. Henry Clay and others denounced the war. John Calhoun said it was unconstitutional because it was begun without a congressional declaration of war. A congressional resolution repeated the charge of unconstitutionality. Calhoun said, "There is no war, according to the sense of our Constitution," because Congress had not initially adopted a formal declaration of war. Newspapers urged immediate withdrawal. But after the Battle of Buena Vista, the same Whig journals hailed the "brilliant war," and General Taylor was chosen as the Whig candidate for President.

The Civil War, as we all know, was even more turbulent in these respects. President Lincoln was badgered by both hawks and doves. In 1863, *The New York Times* said that all that could save the North was immediate negotiation. It urged the appointment of a commission to negotiate with Jefferson Davis. In the spring of 1863, New York was convulsed by draft riots. Homes and buildings were burned; pitched battles were fought between police and rioters; over a thousand people were killed or wounded. A prominent congressman in the fall of 1863 echoed widespread sentiment in the North. He said, "Stop fighting. Make an armistice. Accept at once foreign mediation." A powerful movement began to force Lincoln not to stand for re-election. In August, 1864, Lincoln himself wrote that "this administration will not be re-elected," and the Democratic party nominated General McClellan on a platform pledging that "immediate efforts be made for a cessation of hostilities . . . on the basis of a Federal Union of States."

World War I was strongly supported after Germany's declaration of unrestricted submarine warfare on January 29, 1917. But, even so, the left was vocal and tireless in its opposition. In World War II, isolationist sentiment in the country was strong, well-financed, and well-led until Pearl Harbor. It involved not only the right but also, after the Nazi-Soviet pact, the left. After Pearl Harbor, the country was fairly united.

The Korean War showed the familiar pattern: initial enthusiasm was followed by reaction, frustration, and criticism as time went on and the war was not won. In June, 1950, the

Gallup poll found 81 percent favorable to Truman and the war. But after the initial defeats by the Chinese, a majority of the American people believed the intervention was a mistake, and felt that we should pull out. The Gallup poll showed a profound change of opinion: 66 percent for a pullout. By the spring of 1952, President Truman's popularity, according to the polls, had dropped from 81 percent to 26 percent.

Senator Taft branded the Korean conflict as "an utterly useless war." Senator Wherry said that Dean Acheson "has the blood of our boys in Korea on his hands." . . . Doves demanded withdrawal. . . . Truman was accused of news suppression. . . . Hawks condemned Truman's insistence upon a limited war. . . . But then, somehow, we were able to come through with success in achieving our limited objective of repelling the Communist aggression and enabling the creation of an independent South Korea. It cost us over 150,000 casualties. It took us more than three years. But I think it is fairly universal opinion in the Western world that the war was a necessary action; that if we had not taken on the sad and heavy burden of repelling the invasion of South Korea, no one else would or could have done so; and that the consequences of our default would have been greatly to increase the peril to the non-Communist nations of the world—including ourselves.

I do not cite any of this to denigrate the sincerity or integrity of those who oppose serving in combat roles in Vietnam for profound, moral reasons. It would be beside the point to argue that their judgment is questionable. The point that I make is that where their moral objection is solely to combat service in this particular war, it is not within the doctrine or theory of conscientious objection; and that it would indeed be difficult—perhaps anomalous—perhaps impossible—for the state to acknowledge moral objection to a particular war as a basis for determining draft status, as distinguished from a general religious belief or moral code which rejects all wars.

☆

The Nuremberg Doctrine

REFERENCE IS OFTEN MADE TO THE NUREMBERG
trials which resulted in the punishment of a
number of military officials and civilians for
their participation in the Nazi outrages before
and during World War II. These trials, or more
accurately the London Agreement of August 8,
1945, establishing The International Military
Tribunal to conduct the trials and stating the
principles of adjudication to be followed, are
cited in support of the argument that an individual's personal judgment as to the war in Vietnam should determine his draft status. The
argument is that Nuremberg established the
principle that the individual is legally and morally responsible for his participation in a war,
although he may have acted under superior
orders. If this is so, it is urged, the right of the
individual to refuse to participate should be
acknowledged.

[95]

This argument stretches the theory of the Nuremberg trials.

It is true that the London Agreement provided that the fact that an individual acted under orders should not free him from responsibility. It could be considered only in mitigation of punishment. But the crimes for which punishment might be imposed, despite some looseness of phrasing, were considered to be those that could be committed only by persons who had substantial freedom of choice. It was also the theory of most of the participating nations that only persons who had substantial freedom of choice should be called as defendants to answer for their conduct. It was not considered that the private or the noncommissioned or junior commissioned officer, could be held guilty for carrying out orders issued to him in the ordinary prosecution of war.

The crimes for which persons were brought to trial at Nuremberg, briefly stated, were: (1) crimes against peace, defined as planning, preparing, initiating, or waging a war of aggression; (2) crimes of war, defined as violations of the laws or customs of war; (3) crimes against humanity, defined to include murder, extermination, enslavement, deportation, and other inhuman acts committed against any civilian population. The classes of individuals who were to be held accountable were those who were directly responsible for the "crimes," together with "leaders, organizers, instigators and accomplices."

One may disapprove of the London Agreement and the Nuremberg trials. It is argued that they debased the idea of justice because they rested upon newly defined crimes which were far more exacting and specific than any precedents permitted, because the crimes so created were applied retroactively, and because a truly fair trial was impossible in the circumstances. In defense of the trials, it is urged that there is a basis for them in the International Rules of Law prohibiting acts of barbarism or brutality, that they served an educational purpose for the general public, and that they also assured fairness in the assessment of guilt of the individuals brought to trial.

In any event, it's stretching the point to say that the Nuremberg principle supports the individual's refusal to submit to induction for service in a war which he considers immoral and unjustified. Certainly, that was far from the minds of the representatives of the victorious nations who participated in drafting and approving the

London Agreement and in conducting the trials. They thought that they were directing their efforts only at punishing those who willingly participated in extreme outrages, such as the deliberate murder of civilian population, apart from that which is always incidental to war. For example, they would have been startled if it had been suggested that the principles of Nuremberg made war criminals of the allied command responsible for bombing German cities and destroying their urban population, or for the use of flame throwers in the Japanese command.

Perhaps the time will come when criminal penalties will extend impartially to all killing in all wars so that no one would fight. But this possibility is remote from the still-hostile world in which we live.

CONCLUSION

☆

*"I consider that Constitution as the
rock of our political salvation,
which has preserved us from misery,
division and civil wars; and which
will yet preserve us if we value it rightly
and support it firmly."*
—JOHN MARSHALL

☆

THE STORY OF MAN IS THE HISTORY, FIRST, OF THE
acceptance and imposition of restraints necessary
to permit communal life; and second, of the
emancipation of the individual within that
system of necessary restraints.

Conflict between the demands of ordered
society and the desires and aspirations of the
individual is the common theme of life's development. We find it in the family, where,
first, the child is disciplined to accommodate
himself to the needs of living with others; and
then, as the years go by, he begins the painful
process of achieving for himself relative freedom
of action and a separate identity.

The same is true in any organized society.
The achievement of liberty is man's indispen-
sable condition of living; and yet, liberty cannot

[101]

exist unless it is restrained and restricted. The instrument of balancing these two conflicting factors is the law.

So we must end as we began, with an acknowledgment that the rule of law is the essential condition of individual liberty as it is of the existence of the state.

We are now in the throes of a vast revolution. Considering its scope and depth, it has been relatively peaceful; I think that, even as of today, it is the most profound and pervasive revolution ever achieved by substantially peaceful means.

We have confessed that about twenty million people—Negroes—have been denied the rights and opportunities to which they are entitled. This national acknowledgment—typically American—is in itself a revolutionary achievement.

We have proclaimed our national obligation to repair the damage that this denial has inflicted. We have made a beginning—an important, substantial beginning—in the long, difficult, and enormously costly and disrupting task of reparation and reform.

At the same time, we have faced the revolt of the youth-generation. Our young people have dramatically challenged the authority of their elders. They have asserted the right of the youth-generation to frame its own standards and to a share of power in society.

For the United States, this assertion by the youth-generation of independence and of a claim to authority is relatively new and shocking. In a sense, it has been more disturbing than the Negro revolution to which it is dynamically related.

We have precedents for the trials and disorders that attend the economic and political breakthrough of a segment of the population. But the breakup of patterns of authority—of the straight line of march—is new. Our prior experience of youth's rebellion has been limited to explosions within the pattern. Presently, the design itself is challenged.

In both the Negro and the youth rebellions, the critical question is one of method, of procedure. The definition of objectives and the selection of those which will triumph are of fundamental importance to the quality of our society, of our own lives, and those of our descendants. But the survival of our society as a free, open, democratic community, will be determined not so much by the specific points achieved by the Negroes and the youth-generation as by the procedures—the rules of conduct, the methods, the practices—which survive the confrontations.

Procedure is the bone structure of a democratic society; and the quality of procedural standards which meet general acceptance—the quality of what is tolerable and permissible and acceptable conduct—determines the durability of the society and the survival possibilities of freedom within the society.

I have emphasized that our scheme of law affords great latitude for dissent and opposition. It compels wide tolerance not only for their expression but also for the organization of people and forces to bring about the acceptance of the dissenter's claim. Both our institutions and the characteristics of our national behavior make it possible for opposition to be translated into policy, for dissent to prevail. We have alternatives to violence.

Our present problems emerged as the result of militance and aggressiveness by the Negroes in pressing their dissent and demand. The forcefulness of their activity, in extent and depth, was new to our experience. The fundamental justice of their demands led to a national response, and produced substantial successes. These, in turn, fed the fires of dissent.

The disclosures of national discrimination against the Negroes and neglect of their demands, the example of their tactics, and the successes achieved, both stimulated and inspired the youth-generation. Enough young people had participated in the Negro revolution to provide a nucleus of activists for the youth revolt.

The youth-generation (except, of course, Negro youth) did not have specific grievances comparable to those of the Negroes; but they were stimulated to revolt by a breakup of established patterns in the arts and sciences; by the decline of the institution of the family; by the removal of most of the practical hazards of sex; and by the rude shattering of idealistic conceptions about their nation as a classless society in which all persons, regardless of race, were assured of basic rights and opportunity.

The war in Vietnam and the draft focused their anxieties and fears and their desperate hunger.

It would be idle and foolish to expect that these dissident groups—the Negroes and the youth-generation—would confine themselves to the polite procedures that the other segments of our society would wish. We can hardly claim that their deserving demands would be satisfied if they did not vigorously assert them. We certainly cannot claim that those demands would be satisfied just as soon without their strenuous insistence. But we can, I think, require that the methods which they adopt be within the limits which an organized, democratic society can endure.

An organized society cannot and will not long endure personal and property damage, whatever the reason, context, or occasion.

An organized society will not endure invasion of private premises or public offices, or interference with the work or activities of others if adequate facilities for protest and demonstration are otherwise available.

A democratic society should and must tolerate criticism, protest, demand for change, and organizations and demonstrations within the generally defined limits of the law to marshal support for dissent and change. It should and must make certain that facilities and protection where necessary are provided for these activities.

Protesters and change-seekers must adopt methods within the limits of the law. Despite the inability of anyone always to be certain of

the line between the permissible and the for-
bidden, as a practical matter the lines are reasonably clear.

Violence must not be tolerated; damage to
persons or property is intolerable. Any mass
demonstration is dangerous, although it may be
the most effective constitutional tool of dissent.
But it must be kept within the limits of its
permissible purpose. The functions of mass demonstrations, in the city or on the campus, are
to communicate a point of view; to arouse enthusiasm and group cohesiveness among participants; to attract others to join; and to impress
upon the public and the authorities the point
advocated by the protesters, the urgency of their
demand, and the power behind it. These functions do not include terror, riot, or pillage.

We must accept the discomforts necessarily
implicit in a large, *lawful* demonstration because, in a sense, it is part of the dynamics of
democracy which depends for its vitality upon
the vigorous confrontation of opposing forces.
But we cannot and should not endure physical
assault upon person or property. This sort of
assault is ultimately counter-productive. It po-
larizes society, and in any polarization, the
minority group, although it may achieve initial,

limited success, is likely to meet bitter reprisal and rejection of its demands.

In my judgment civil disobedience—the deliberate violation of law—is never justified in our nation, where the law being violated is not itself the focus or target of the protest. So long as our governments obey the mandate of the Constitution and assure facilities and protection for the powerful expression of individual and mass dissent, the disobedience of laws which are not themselves the target of the protest—the violation of law merely as a technique of demonstration—constitutes an act of rebellion, not merely of dissent.

Civil disobedience is violation of law. Any violated of law must be punished, whatever its purpose, as the theory of civil disobedience recognizes. But law violation directed not to the laws or practices that are the subject of dissent, but to unrelated laws which are disobeyed merely to dramatize dissent, may be morally as well as politically unacceptable.

At the beginning of this discussion, I presented the dilemma of obedience to law and the need that sometimes may arise to disobey profoundly immoral or unconstitutional laws. This is another kind of civil disobedience, and the only kind that, in my view, is ever truly defensible as a matter of social morality.

It is only in respect to such laws—laws that are basically offensive to fundamental values of life or the Constitution—that a moral (although not a legal) defense of law violation can possibly be urged. Anyone assuming to make the judgment that a law is in this category assumes a terrible burden. He has undertaken a fearful moral as well as legal responsibility. He should be prepared to submit to prosecution by the state for the violation of law and the imposition of punishment if he is wrong or unsuccessful. He should even admit the correctness of the state's action in seeking to enforce its laws, and he should acquiesce in the ultimate judgment of the courts.

For after all, each of us is a member of an organized society. Each of us benefits from its existence and its order. And each of us must be ready, like Socrates, to accept the verdict of its institutions if we violate their mandate and our challenge is not vindicated.

Animating all of this in our society is the principle of tolerance. The state must tolerate the individual's dissent, appropriately expressed. The individual must tolerate the majority's verdict when and as it is settled in accordance with the laws and the procedures that have been established. Dissent and dissenters have no monopoly on freedom. They must tolerate opposition. They must accept dissent from their dissent. And they must give it the respect and the latitude which they claim for themselves. Neither youth nor virtue can justify the disregard of this principle, in the classroom, the public hall, or on the streets. Protest does not justify hooliganism.

These are workable, viable principles in our nation, for we have alternatives to violence and alternatives to suppression. For the state, our constitutional principles, although they provide wide latitude for demonstration and dissent, permit strong and effective state response to violence. For the citizen, the guarantee of freedom of speech, of press, of peaceable assembly, of protest, of organization and dissent provides powerful instruments for effecting change. And ultimately, the all-important power of the vote —access to the ballot box—furnishes the most effective weapon in the citizen's arsenal.

The experience of these past few years shows, more vividly than any other episode in our history, how effective these alternatives are.

It is through their use—and not through the sporadic incidents of violence—that we have effected the current social revolution; and it is through their use that we have begun to create a new and—hopefully—richer and better set of institutions and attitudes.

In short, we have shown that our democratic processes do indeed function, and that they can bring about fundamental response to fundamental demands, and can do this without revolution, and despite the occasional violence of those who either reject or have not attained the maturity and restraint to use, and not to abuse, their freedom. This is an extraordinary tribute to our institutions.

ABOUT THE AUTHOR

Abe Fortas was born in Memphis, Tennessee, in 1910. He received his A.B. from Southwestern College and his LL.B from Yale in 1933. While there he was editor in chief of the *Yale Law Journal*. He has been a member of the Yale University School of Law faculty, Under Secretary of the Interior, advisor to the U.S. delegation to the United Nations in San Francisco and London, and a member of the law firm of Arnold, Fortas and Porter.

On July 28, 1965, he was nominated Associate Justice of the Supreme Court of the United States by President Lyndon B. Johnson.